THE TRUTH
OF THE
MATTER
Stemilt's Founding Father

Thomas Kyle Mathison

Joni Cipriano Pepperl

STEMILT GROWERS, INC.

WENATCHEE, WA

This book is dedicated to the memory of Tom Mathison in order to inspire family, friends, and the fruit industry he served.

– The Mathison Family

Contents

Chapter 1

The Dam Breaks

There are pivotal moments in a person's life, moments that mark life-altering changes.

These moments are never planned. They cannot be predicted or directed. But when they occur, a life is never again the same. A path that might have gone one way is forever changed. In one crystal-clear second, a destiny begins.

For Thomas Kyle Mathison, a young man just back from serving his country in a devastating world war, that moment came on February 16, 1947.

It started innocently enough. The Sunday dawned bright and clear, with sunshine creating sparkling diamonds in the snow. Children ran outside to play in

the puddles. Families left for church in good spirits, enjoying the break from the heavy snow that had pummeled the valley that winter. By afternoon, the temperature soared to a balmy 65 degrees Fahrenheit and a warm wind was blowing. Old-man winter was finally

FAMILY TIME – The Mathison family poses for a picture.

loosening his grip, and the town was ready to celebrate.

But the mood was anything but celebratory at the Mathison homestead on Stemilt Hill. Chris Mathison, Tom's father, had built a pond on the ranch the summer before, but had not been able to complete the spillway which would have taken excess water out of the pond without washing out the dam. There was always one chore or another taking up his time and, as hard as he worked, he would go to bed at night with a list of tasks still undone. The spillway was one of many, but with the cold winter the valley had been experiencing, it hardly seemed likely the pond would be going anywhere soon. That is, until the cruel heat of that lovely Sunday.

Chris ran to the pond and, in utter dismay, quickly saw what this unfinished chore was going to cost. Water was spilling everywhere, in rushing torrents that were oddly out of place with the normally dry surroundings. Without a spillway in place, the dam was in jeopardy of failing. "Grab hay bales!" he screamed to Tom. "Shore up the dam!"

Tom dashed to work, hauling bale after bale of hay, in an effort to stem the flow. He worked feverishly alongside his father, running back and forth to the hay bales, hauling them to the pond, and trying to shore up the terrible force of water gone wild. The sun mocked their efforts and the warm breeze lapped at the melting snow.

Suddenly, while Tom and Chris were balancing precariously on the dam, each carrying huge bales of hay, the entire structure gave way, sending both of them into

QUALITY TIME WITH DAD –
Tom and his father, Chris, pictured
together during happier times.

the frigid waters. Gasping for air, Tom managed to pull his head above water and grab the side of the bank. With intense effort, he inched himself up until he could gain a better grip. Using every ounce of strength he had, he pulled himself up and over the bank, coughing out water and heaving great gulps of air into his lungs.

He shook his head to clear his thoughts. "Dad?" he creaked. "Dad? Dad!"

His cries took on a new urgency. His father was still in the water!

He tried, over and over again, to locate his father in the muddy depths. Sheer panic ran through every cell in his body, and he desperately tried to do the impossible—first find his Dad and then try to pull him out. Screaming wildly for help that didn't come, it was a losing battle.

Chris drowned that day. And Tom's life was never the same.

Chapter 2

Early Years

THE THIRD GENERATION – The picture above, with proud parents Chris and Adelaide holding the twins, was taken in 1926 and is one of the earliest photos of Tom.

Tom was born on June 23, 1926 into a busy farm household, and was almost overlooked during those first few seconds of life. Ida Slack, a neighbor and midwife assisting in the delivery, was intent on doing her job—she had just delivered Tom's mother of a healthy girl, soon named Helen. As she was cleaning up this new bundle of joy, she happened to look down and, to her shock, saw something unusual.

"Oh, my God, there's another one!" she screamed. Sure enough, Thomas Kyle Mathison came kicking and screaming into the world. After cleaning him up, the midwife put him in a shoe box and stashed him in the open oven to keep him warm. In later years, Tom would often joke that life, for him, started in the oven as if he were nothing more than a warm biscuit.

Tom joined two older siblings, both with wildly different personalities. Older brother, Ray Atwood Mathison, enjoyed his firstborn status. "I always thought he was spoiled," Tom said. "He got whatever he wanted—in fact, he got to drive the family car to high school."

IN THE ORCHARD – Even as toddlers, Tom and his twin sister, Helen, were inseparable. This picture was taken near the Mathison family orchard in the summer of 1927.

Sister Mary was a quiet, independent person, with a mellow temperament. She moved to Berkeley when she got older, to stay with Aunt Estelle and go to business school. Afterwards, she joined the U.S. Army.

Sadly, Tom never got to meet his sister, Margaret. She was born two years before him, but lived only a few days.

Luckily for Tom and his sister, Helen, they were both blessed with strong constitutions. "Helen was taller than I was," he recalled. "She had red hair and a temper to match. I remember getting beat up by her a few times, but mostly, we got along fine."

Life on the farm was often hard, and Tom was expected to pull his weight at a young age. His particular responsibility revolved around the cows. The family had nine of them, and Tom's job was to feed the calves. "I'd teach the small ones to drink milk out of a bucket," he remembered.

THE EARLY YEARS – The Mathison kids celebrating Tom and Helen's first birthday in June 1927. From left to right: Helen, Mary, and Tom.

He learned how to separate the cream from the milk, and how to make butter—all important skills his family depended on for survival. "Mother sold the butter, and Dad would buy the calves for $5, then grow them up and break them to milk," he remembered. "When they were pregnant with their second calf, he would sell them back to the dairies."

The cows were just one part of his busy day. He was also responsible for feeding the chickens, gathering the eggs, and cleaning the chicken coop, the latter being an unpleasant task on any day, but especially so on those dark mornings before heading to school.

School wasn't Tom's crowning achievement. He walked a mile on those mornings to a small school that is now the Stemilt Grange Hall. In the bitter winter, his Dad would sometimes hook up the horses and plow the snow off the road to make it a little easier for the children to get to school. "Colleen and Bill Woods lived down the road about a quarter of a mile, and they would walk to school with us," Tom remembered.

There were eight grades, with 29 students in total. "Miss Whitehall was the teacher, and she graduated from Ellensburg," Tom recalled. "She had a hard time controlling and disciplining the kids. There were great big boys in the 7th and 8th grade who were six feet tall."

Tom was a slow learner and, though his mother would try to help him with his homework, she'd get upset when he stumbled with his reading. The situation worsened for Tom when the Stemilt Hill School consolidated with the South Wenatchee School. Now he had to ride a bus of sorts each morning—actually the back of a 1932 pickup truck with plywood that held wooden benches rattling all the way on the washboard road. It's a wonder the children made it to school with teeth and limbs intact. If it wasn't for his best friend, Cliff Daniels, he would have been sorely tempted to skip school altogether.

BOY AND GIRL PATROL – One of Tom's proudest accomplishments in school was being named Chief Patrol Boy in the 8th grade. Tom, pictured above with the flag, said this honor did a lot to boost his self confidence.

A big break happened in 8th grade, though, and it made all the difference. Mr. Adrien Douglas, a teacher and principal of South Wenatchee School, boosted Tom's self-confidence. "He called me into his office one day and told me I was going to be chief patrol boy for the whole school year," Tom said. "The patrol got to wear red jackets with white shoulder straps!"

That uniform of distinction did more for Tom's learning abilities than anything up to that point. He realized he was about two years behind the other students in his grade, so he enrolled in summer school to catch up. He managed to pass the state exam and move on to junior high school. "I passed, but only by one percent," he remembered. "The other boys in the 'dumb room' were sent on to 9th grade, too, but only if they could keep up because, like me, they were behind most of the others."

The "dumb boys", as Tom called them, managed to all end up in Miss Ross's first period English class, a tremendously lucky break. She decided she would make it her mission to see that they all made it through junior high. She arranged her schedule to have an open period each day to meet with them, and tutor them individually and collectively. As a result, all went on to high school.

PANTHER SPORTS – In high school, Tom was #37 on the Wenatchee High Panthers football team. The team went undefeated in 1944 and only had one touchdown scored against them.

"I enjoyed my high school years and got decent grades," Tom said. "I played football in the Cross-State League, and played all over the state. I remember beating Bremerton on a muddy field. They were supposed to be the best team in the state, but we beat them 27-0. Cle Elem scored the only touchdown against us, but we still beat them 66-6."

Whether it was school work, farming, or football, Tom simply did what needed to be done, and didn't expect life to be easy. It certainly wasn't for his forefathers. Grandpa Thomas Kyle Mathison and his family immigrated from the Isle of Lewis in Scotland to Nova Scotia, Canada when he was an infant. At age 12, he was employed as a cabin boy. He eventually wound up on a ship that sailed around the horn of South America to California. "Grandpa Tom was said to have a hard Scottish brogue, and few could understand him," Tom said. "As a boy, he spoke Gaelic at home."

It didn't stop the older Mathison from meeting and marrying Helen Atwood, though. She lived in Madera, California, where her family grew table grapes. In 1890, they made their way north to Washington. Along the way, she had a son—born in a blockhouse in Goldendale. That son was Chris Atwood Mathison, Tom's Dad. Later, a daughter, Estelle Carney Mathison, would join their little family.

HORSING AROUND – Mary, Tom, and Helen pose with their pal, Teddy the Horse, circa 1936.

As the young family continued north, they stopped short in Wenatchee. "It reminded my Grandpa of the hills in Scotland," Tom said. So, it was a natural progression for his grandfather to end up on Stemilt Hill.

Without water on the new homestead, it was very difficult to eke out a living. Drinking water had to be hauled from Stemilt Creek in barrels. Later, a cistern was put in, and then a pipe running to the house. "For irrigation water, Grandpa Tom dug a ditch by hand, with the help of a horse and plow, to the creek to deliver water from the spring runoff," Tom said. "It filled ponds on the ranch, and irrigated the small orchard and field crops they had."

Grandma Helen died in 1908 and was buried on Stemilt Hill, changing the lives of Chris and Estelle drastically. Estelle was sent to California to live with an aunt. Chris went to Iowa to attend accounting school.

Though the following years are sketchy in detail, one can only imagine the hardness of life that stretched ahead for Grandpa Thomas. In the icy cold winter of 1922, he was out cutting ice at Three Lakes, and hauling it up Stemilt Hill to fill the icehouse, an arduous task. One night, after a grueling day, he couldn't shake a bad chill. That chill turned into pneumonia, and Grandpa Tom died that winter.

That left the farm to Chris and Estelle, and Chris was a natural for taking it over. "It's been said many times that the man had no fear," Tom recalled. "He loved to break wild horses and, one time, a horse bucked out of the corral with Chris on its back. It ran right through the apricot orchard, and hit a limb, scraping Chris off with a thud. Though he had a badly lacerated chin, he just jumped right back on and kept riding."

That wild spirit was matched in a young gal named Adelaide Sherwood who caught his eye. "Dad said many times that when he first saw Ada riding her horse, with her long auburn hair flying in the wind, he decided right then and there that he wanted to marry her," Tom said.

The couple tied the knot in 1914, splurging on a wedding trip to Seattle to stay at the Vance Hotel. Ada was 17 years old at the time.

Originally from Chicago, Ada's family had traveled west after her father was badly injured at his railroad job. There was no such thing as worker's compensation at the time, so he moved his family across the country and started a blacksmith shop.

With that kind of family strength behind her, it's not surprising that Ada turned out to be a working partner to Chris. "She worked the ranch with my Dad, raised the children, and spent her whole life working," Tom said. "She often talked about how she had planned to go to school and become a teacher, and always blamed Chris for coming along and changing those plans!"

Ada was an incredibly strong woman, for her time or any time, and she was a huge force in Tom's life. "She pushed Tom when his confidence was low," West Mathison, Tom's grandson, says. "As a young person, someone needs to believe in you for you to become successful. Ada was that source of strength for Tom."

Chapter 3

Going to War

The best-laid plans do have a tendency to change. Tom's busy childhood of chores, school, football, and family life came to an abrupt halt one day when he got his notice to report to the U.S. Army.

BEFORE DEPLOYMENT – Tom and his family pose for a picture just before Tom's deployment to Japan.

Tom was eager and ready to go. He had actually registered a year earlier, but was needed on the farm for one more harvest. In 1945, he was sent to Camp Roberts with other young recruits for 15 weeks of training. "I found myself in sick call because my wisdom teeth were hurting," Tom remembered. "The dentist decided to take all four of them out and said, 'Kid, you're going to be sick for a while.'"

Tom quickly discovered that, sick or not, the Army didn't slow things down. When he got back to his barracks, everyone was rolling up their gear in preparation for a 3:00 a.m. departure to the Pacific front. "I was bleeding badly and my face was swollen," he said. "A friend, George Kishner, helped me pack my gear. I couldn't even open my mouth."

His troop walked five miles to a barge to get to their ship in San Francisco. "I couldn't eat and I was really hurting," Tom said. "A Red Cross woman gave me a cup of coffee and I never tasted anything so good!"

It was a rough crossing and, oddly enough, Tom's sore mouth might have helped him avoid seasickness. "Everyone got sick, but me," he remembered. "The bunks were five high and I was on the bottom bunk. Even the doctor who removed my stitches was seasick."

JOINING THE ARMY – Tom was in Tokyo Bay for the signing of the armistice when the war ended.

Tom arrived first in Manila and later in Japan. During that time, he learned a lot about self-discipline. "I was promoted to staff sergeant and I had to manage people," he said. "I saw a lot of people who were mismanaged by arrogance and poor management style. I learned what not to do, as much as anything."

ARMY LIFE - Like any young soldier, Tom had many unique life experiences while at war.

Tom was assigned to the 43rd Infantry division and the 172nd Infantry regiment. His assignment—track down the Japanese in Northern Luzon who were holding out in caves. The danger was obvious. On his way to the next assignment—to go to Okinawa to prepare for the invasion of Japan—he was met with the best news he could imagine. Japan had surrendered!

Tom remained in Japan, assigned to a special detachment that supplied drinking water and supplies to the troops. He drove a weapons carrier over 21,000 miles during that time, covering every part of the area.

In one of his first entrepreneurial moves, he also started a night club with two friends on the roof of an office building in downtown Tokyo. They named it the Starlight Café. The trio focused on serving the GIs who were left to help rebuild Tokyo. They served Japanese beer and played American music. Tom recounts that "we were doing a big business." It soon bloomed into an open air dance hall.

Of the three guys who started the Starlight, Tom was the first called home as his tour of duty ended. The partners

SPECIAL ASSIGNMENT - Once the war ended, Tom was reassigned to the 1st Calvary division with the 8th Engineers.

HOME FROM WAR – Tom and his mother, AJ, photographed near the family car upon his return home from war in 1946.

offered Tom $10,000 for his share of the business, and he was quite pleased with their offer. The experience ignited an entrepreneurial spirit which would carry him on to many more successful ventures.

When he was released to go home, in a final irony, his troop ship encountered a massive typhoon with waves reaching 100 feet. "I'll tell you what," Tom said in his deadpan way, "that was an experience to remember the rest of my life."

Son Kyle thinks the war experience shaped Tom's management style. "Douglas MacArthur, commander of the U.S. armed forces in the Pacific, was one of the most influential people to my Dad," Kyle says. "Douglas MacArthur was kind of a dictatorship-type leader, and that's the way it was. When Stemilt got too big too fast in the 1970's and 1980's, Tom got back to basics and showed that same management style. I was named after Douglas MacArthur (my middle name is Douglas), and I really appreciate it."

Tom also took some risks in his career that Kyle attributes directly to his war years. "People ask how he could take some of the risks he did with the company, but I think it comes back to his time during World War II," Kyle says. "He was fighting in these islands, dug into a foxhole and keeping himself low, while shots were flying and guys were dying right and left. He made a pact with God that, if he ever got out alive, he would never complain about anything."

Tom got out and felt he had been given a second chance. "He could gamble because he got out with his life," Kyle notes.

Tom realized that, in a strange way, the war provided him with an odd gift. "My own Dad was a worrier," Tom said. "He worried about everything and he had plenty to worry about. He would worry if the rain was going to hit the cherries and he would just pace the floor. I realized that, if I was lucky enough to get home safely, I would look forward to having those kinds of worries. No matter what happened later, I always remembered that."

Chapter 4

Early Fruit

Spring of 1947 was Tom's season to take on the farm full force, and the challenges kept mounting.

His brother, Ray, worked by his side, but Ray had contracted polio in 1945 and it was becoming increasingly difficult for him to do the heavy labor. "Ray was the star kid growing up," says Lavonne Mathison van Someren Gréve, Tom's daughter. "He was extremely athletic and very smart. When he got polio, it changed everything."

HARD-WORKING BROTHERS – Tom and his older brother, Ray, shown here taking a break while working together on the family farm.

Tom, Ray, and neighbors Joe Bainard and Charlie Woods at first all worked for Tom's mother, Adelaide, for the princely sum of $1.00 per hour. They planted a pear orchard and put in a pipeline to the Stemilt Irrigation District box, back-breaking labor under a scorching hot sun. "1947 was clear and warm all summer," Tom said. "It was one of the earliest seasons ever. We finished Lamberts on July 3rd, much earlier than normal."

Eventually, Joe's son, Gene, joined in, and the extended Bainard family worked with the Mathison family for the next three generations.

Tom sold the 1947 cherry crop to A.Z. Wells, who paid him 16-cents per pound for 12-row and larger, with culls out. Though Tom and crew picked 125 tons, the market was a "disaster," according to Tom, "and A.Z. lost a lot of money."

That same year, Ray took a job with the Bureau of Reclamation as an auditor on the Columbia Basin Project. Tom meanwhile found time to attend government-funded horticulture classes, learning details about fruit trees that would add to his quickly expanding knowledge base.

In spite of his desire to keep learning and improving, Tom was destined to suffer setback after setback during those early years. The summer of 1949 brought five severe rainstorms immediately followed by several 100-degree days, taking its toll on the quality of the crop. "It was another big cherry crop and there was no cash market," Tom said. "We ended up consigning the crop to J. M. Wade, getting five-cents a pound for 11-row and larger, and three-cents a pound for 12-row which was about half the crop. We spent about three-quarters of a cent per pound for picking and didn't receive enough to cover our expenses."

MOTHER AND SON – Tom admired his mother for her strength and as the matriarch of the Mathison family.

The winter of 1949-1950 was the coldest on record, reaching 28 degrees below zero at one point. "We had extensive damage and lost our cherry trees," Tom remembered. The following winter brought more of the same extreme weather, and the Mathisons were forced to watch as their orchards suffered and returns plummeted.

The failing fruit crop was not the only hardship the family had to endure. Adelaide, once a strong and vibrant woman, was suffering from a variety of health ailments, often to the point where she could barely function. She grew steadily worse, and Tom and his siblings were at a loss to find a solution. Finally, in the spring of 1949, she suffered a full-blown nervous breakdown.

Tom attributed the state of her health to stress over the death of his father, and the mounting pressures of sustaining the family farm. "We took her to the Ferlon Sanitarium in Seattle for a few months," Tom said. "When she returned home, she was still sick, but finally completely recovered to become the matriarch of the entire Mathison family for the next 30 years."

Though Tom used few words to sum up the situation, it doesn't take much imagination to picture how his mother's poor health must have affected his own role in the family. In short order, Tom became the strong shoulders everyone would lean on, not only to run the family farm, but for the family's basic survival. He took on the role without complaint, just focusing instead on getting the job done. He eventually purchased all shares of the farm from his mother and siblings.

The same kind of resilience that allowed Adelaide to return to full functioning also ran in Tom's blood, and it kept him plugging away at every obstacle, creating hope and looking forward to better times.

It pushed him to improve himself in every way, including working hard to improve his self-confidence. He took a Dale Carnegie course every Wednesday night to learn to overcome his fear of speaking in public. Little steps led to bigger ones, and as time went on, Tom sat on every major apple, pear, and cherry board, holding leadership positions in most of them. The humble man

THE BUSINESSMAN – Soon after taking the reigns of the family business, Tom enrolled in a speech course and government-funded horticulture class. Tom often represented the tree fruit industry within the state and national government.

from Stemilt Hill, who dreaded public speaking, found himself representing the Washington apple industry at an economic roundtable conference, sitting next to Vice President Al Gore and chatting with President Bill Clinton. Somewhere along the way, Tom definitely found his voice.

Chapter 5

Lorraine Takes Center Stage

If you're lucky in life, you find a partner to share your joys, your disappointments, and the plain day-to-day business of living. Tom found his partner in 1949, when a friend insisted he drive to Coulee Dam to enjoy a picnic and get to know a certain young lady.

This was no ordinary lady. France Lorraine Goldy had just graduated from Washington State University and was a woman ahead of her time. She came from a farming family in the Palisades and was no stranger to hard work. Her parents, Lillian and Bob, both served in World War I. Bob had the misfortune of being gassed during the war, but the good fortune to meet Lillian, who worked for the Red Cross. They named their only daughter after a place they had both been in the war—Lorraine, France.

Tom knew who Lorraine was—they had both attended Wenatchee High School, though their paths didn't cross too often. Her parents' ranch was a long trek from Wenatchee High School. To make it easier for her to get her education, it was decided that she would live and work in Wenatchee during her junior high and high school years. She worked at the Porch School Store during high school, and Tom was a customer. He would come in to buy pencils and tablet paper, which was probably an excuse to briefly chat with Lorraine.

She did remember him—mainly because he always wore a crisp, ironed shirt, and that impressed her. "I think his twin sister, Helen, did his ironing because she liked him looking nice," Lorraine recalls.

Lorraine went on to gain her degree in sociology, quite a feat for a woman at that time. It wasn't long before her determination landed her a great job—clear across the country in Lima, Ohio, where she worked with the YWCA planning educational events for girls at three area high schools (similar to today's mentoring programs). She didn't start until the fall, so it gave Tom one summer to try to win her over before she was to leave.

Lorraine's cousin, Thena Steffen, most likely started the ball rolling when she and her husband, John, planned that picnic at Grand Coulee Dam, inviting both Tom and Lorraine along. This blind date was their first real date, and it made an impression.

In Tom's words: "That summer, I called on her, though she had several other admirers. She went to Lima at the end of the summer, but I just kept writing letters until she finally decided to come back to Wenatchee."

We'll have to read between the lines, but those must have been great letters. Son Bob later says, "Their letters typically consisted of sharing the events of each other's day. Tom would talk about a sprayer he was building, while Lorraine would talk about the young girls she was helping to grow into strong women. They also talked frequently about how they would fit into each other's lives."

It was a natural fit. Lorraine knew all about ranch life and the long hours it took just to survive. She was confident she could handle the challenges of that life. In

fact, when she was a very young girl, a friend of her parents commented once that Lorraine would make a great cherry grower's wife. "I guess it was always in the back of my mind," Lorraine laughs.

Tom convinced Lorraine that the right time had come to marry. Knowing that Tom wasn't about to move to Ohio, she resigned from her job and moved back to Wenatchee in the winter of 1949 to plan their wedding.

LONG-DISTANCE LOVE – This is Tom and Lorraine's engagement picture, taken in 1950.

Tom knew they would need a car and, because of the expense of that, he was planning to save a bit of money by skipping the purchase of a ring. Lorraine let him know loud and clear that a wedding ring was a definite necessity.

"So, O.K., I needed a car and a wedding ring," Tom said. "Leroy Burton, the town jeweler, sold me a quarter-carat diamond ring and a 1941 Mercury Coupe for $1,500."

Not a bad deal! Tom and Lorraine were married on March 8, 1950 in the Calvary Presbyterian Church on First Street in Wenatchee. They spent the first night of their honeymoon in Everett, and then traveled on to Victoria, British Columbia for a relaxing week to start their marriage together. Lorraine drove the car a bit on that trip, but didn't have her glasses. Tom wisely decided he would be the driver from then on.

GETTING MARRIED – Tom and Lorraine were married on March 8, 1950 at the Calvary Church in a ceremony officiated by each of their childhood ministers, Herb Schulz and Frank Baity.

It was the most relaxed they would be for years, because things changed quickly when they got back to Wenatchee. "There was 18 inches of snow on the ground," Tom recalled. "I got right to work building a shop, and getting a sprayer and orchard trailer ready for the upcoming season."

Tom and Lorraine rented a small apartment on Douglas Street in Wenatchee that first year, but were able to rent a small house from Lawrence Hedges on Stemilt Hill the following year to be closer to the orchards. "It had a sawdust furnace that was hard to keep running," Tom said. "We still milked cows, fed the chickens, and raised steer."

Tom was a hard worker and put in long hours each day on the farm. The young couple struggled financially, and learned how to live on very little. Even so, Lorraine always said Tom provided very well for her. She made sure he had three square meals a day. "I would eat the jam and he would eat the bread," she says.

GOLDEN ANNIVERSARY – Tom and Lorraine celebrated their 50th wedding anniversary alongside family and friends in 2000.

That same year, Tom began building the family home, with the help of Jess McLaughlin and Gale Richardson. He built it right on the foundation of his father's old house, one that had burnt down. "We built the cupboards, put in the woodwork, and moved in March of the next year," Tom said. "We had an open house full of people, when I noticed that the main floor was sagging."

Tom's solution was to put a couple of 2 x 4's under the sag, which are still there to this day. The tiny two-bedroom, one-bath home kept them safe and warm for years, and they eventually added on to it to accommodate some life changes.

Those changes took the form of three very lively children.

Chapter 6

Growing Mathisons

By far, Tom's proudest moments came in the 1950's.

On August 22, 1951, Robert Carl was born. "Lorraine had a hard delivery," Tom said, "but she could handle it."

Their first-born son was named after Lorraine's father, with his middle name standing for each grandparent—C for Chris, A for Adelaide, R for Robert, and L for Lillian.

One year later, on November 6, Kyle Douglas was born. He was named after Thomas Kyle and Douglas MacArthur, definitely an interesting blend.

On November 19, 1953, the family was complete when Judith Lavonne was born, named Judith after Adelaide (her middle name) and Lavonne because Tom and Lorraine liked the name.

Lorraine spent the next two decades raising the three children, which meant feeding and

A YOUNG FAMILY – In August 1951, Tom and Lorraine welcomed their first child, a son named Robert Carl. By 1953, the Mathisons added two more to their young family – son Kyle Douglas was born in 1952 and daughter Judith Lavonne was born in 1953.

clothing the family through some lean times. Family income rarely exceeded $300 a month plus the cream check, but it didn't stop Lorraine from putting three

square meals on the table every day. She also found time to serve as a Sunday School teacher, 4-H leader, home room parent at school, cherry harvest kid crew boss, and the coordinator of the family schedule, making sure everyone got to school, Little League, Ski School, and so on.

PROUD PAPA – Tom with all three kids near an orchard.

Oldest son, Bob, has plenty of memories of those early years. "Early in the morning, we would all sit down to breakfast together—me in the middle, Kyle next to Daddy, and Lavonne next to Mom," he recalls. "The radio would always be on KPQ, and I can still hear it. Dad would eat breakfast, then walk around the table and give each of us a kiss on the cheek. I remember the stubble of his chin was rough and would put a shiver down my back. We would rub our cheeks to shrug the kiss away. Then he went to work."

BREAK WITH BOYS – Dressed in their Sunday best, Tom, Bob, & Kyle get their photo taken together.

Like clockwork, Tom would be back at noon for dinner, the big meal of the day at that time. "Mom would usually cook fried steaks," Bob recalls. "After eating, Daddy would always lie down on the davenport and we kids would lie down beside him. We would always fidget and squirm, so he would never really be able to sleep. At 1:00 sharp, he was gone."

SUNNY DAY – Tom & Lorraine with family and the family pet.

Bob's memories are clear and specific. "At 6:00, it was suppertime, and Daddy would drive up with yesterday's paper in the mail," he says. "He would either come in the house and read the paper or sit in his truck where it was quiet!"

Supper consisted of sandwiches and soup, and Tom would take the time to connect with his children. "He would ask each of us what we did that day," Bob says. "Of course, we could never remember, so he would ask if

BACK FROM HUNTING – Tom and his three children pose with a deer that Tom got during a hunting trip around 1955.

we learned anything in school. He really wanted to know what we did. Mama always had a dozen or so things to report that she had accomplished that day. He would shake his head and Mama would get defensive."

GOING FOR A RIDE – Tom takes Bob on a ride around the farm.

Tom's supper routine was followed by a brief nap, and then back to work in his office until bedtime. It was a simple routine, steady and regular, and it formed a pattern which defined family life for the children. They knew where their Daddy was, they knew he cared about them, and they knew what to expect from him. In today's hectic pace, it speaks to a time many people long for—the sureness of a father's love, the steadiness of a family's commitment to each other, and the quiet strength that children need to feel secure.

There were treats to look forward to, and they were regular as clockwork, too. "On Saturday night, we would go to Dusty's and have a hamburger and milkshake, eating it in the 1951 Oldsmobile, parked there on Wenatchee Avenue," Bob remembers. "Dad would turn on the radio,

CARS – Tom loved cars and loved driving them even more. Here, Tom and his growing kids pose in front of the family car.

eat his meal, and then finish off what we couldn't eat."

Lavonne recalls regular Sunday drives, but always with a focus. "Dad would load us up in the un-air-conditioned car for what seemed like hours, and take us to look at newly planted orchards," she remembers. "They just looked like sticks in the ground to us, but Dad was excited to show us what other orchardists in the state were doing."

APPLE BLOSSOM – Tom and his daughter Lavonne pictured before heading to Apple Blossom in 1972.

One other weekly event occurred with regularity. "Every Sunday, after church, Mama and Daddy would have a big fight," Bob recalls with glee. "It was as if they had nothing else to do. Dad would always say the roast was overdone, which it usually was, and then the fur would fly. I remember once Mama picked up a tomato and threw it at him. He ducked and it hit the desk behind him. He laughed and thought it was funny, and she stormed out of the house for a couple of hours."

TEENAGE GRANDCHILDREN - Tom with Kyle and his family.

NEW TRUCK – Tom, his children, and several grandchildren pose alongside the family's new truck in 1996.

Tom had special nicknames for his children. Bob was Robby Bob Starfish. Kyle was Pard Douglas. Lavonne was Princess. "I don't know how he came up with these nicknames," Bob says, "but he always said them with love."

Though Lorraine was the day-to-day discipliner ("We'd get at least one spanking a day from her," Bob says), Tom would kick in, if necessary. "If you were unruly at the table," Bob says, "he would pick up his spoon, clean it with a napkin, and hit you on the back of the head with it. Tears would flow and he'd say, 'Quit feeling sorry for yourself.'"

If meals at the Mathison household sound fascinating, imagine the trouble that could happen away from the table. Bob and Kyle had plenty of scuffles, and probably should consider themselves lucky to have escaped childhood in one piece. "I remember one time when Kyle was headed down the hill toward Aunt Jane's house on his bicycle when, all of a sudden, his brakes failed," Bob says. "He hit Aunt Jane's front door so hard that, even though it was closed tight, he knocked it wide open. Aunt Jane came out and just gave him heck for hitting her door and slammed it. Meanwhile, Kyle was lying there unconscious!"

Time with Tom in the field was another exercise in survival, especially when the children tagged along while he did such chores as installing electric fences. "We had to learn how to get through them without being shocked, because Daddy wasn't going to wait for us," Bob says.

Kyle came home white as a ghost one day after tramping behind Tom and Bob. He asked Lorraine, "Do people die if they are electrocuted?"

She assured him they do.

"Kyle didn't say anything for the rest of the day," Bob laughs. "He just sat down quietly and waited to die."

Chapter 7

Showdown

One year stands out among the rest as the year of Lorraine's showdown with Tom.

It was 1958, and the cherry crop was bountiful. Even a hot summer with badly timed rain didn't slow the flow that year, since plenty of cherries avoided splitting.

New York was the biggest and best market, so that's where Tom sent his crop. Though he was using polyliners and market arrival was improving, the sad truth is one whole carload only sold for 36-cents per box. To work that hard, all season long, to barely cover expenses, was a huge blow.

Tom was devastated, and he didn't hide his feelings from the family. He was angry, depressed, and feeling very sorry for himself and his situation.

Finally, Lorraine had enough. "Listen," she told him in no uncertain terms, "I am sick of your attitude! You either find out what you're doing wrong and fix it, or go down to Alcoa and get a job to support this family!"

This ultimatum had just the effect Lorraine intended. Tom may have spent another moment or two lamenting his plight, but the pity party didn't last long.

The next summer, Tom went to the auction market in New York, staying with his sister Mary and riding the subway to the pier on the Hudson River. "They started selling our cherries at 6 in the morning," he remembered. "The brand was 'Boy Blue.' After checking it out, I walked to Lower Manhattan to look at cherries and that's when it hit me. Lorraine was right! There was a definite problem and I better solve it."

It was so simple, Tom couldn't believe the solution had eluded him this long. The cherries were beautiful when they were shipped, but by the time they got to market, they were soft with dry stems and no luster. "That's what we had to fix!" he screamed. It was his Eureka moment.

He went back home and talked to every local grower he knew. He even talked to the growers in other states. He branched out and began talking to anyone who knew anything about growing cherries. He made a game plan of what to do, but no one wanted to spend the money to get it done. "I talked to the Fruit Growers Service and everyone I could think of, but it was obvious that, if this was going to happen, we would have to make the investment on our own," he said.

TRANSFORMING HIS BUSINESS – In June 1960, Tom began construction on his first packing warehouse atop Stemilt Hill, the first of many efforts to improve the quality of his cherries at the marketplace.

So, in 1960, Stemilt embarked on the first of several investments in storing and packing fruit. The company built a 45 x 54-ft. cold storage building, with a polysheet over the top of the cherry lugs, keeping the moisture in and the cherries fresh.

"We filled the storage during the day and then delivered the cherries to Fruit Growers Service to pack the next morning when it was cool," he recalled.

That was just the beginning. The next year, they built an addition to the cold storage, along with a 24 x 112-ft. packing room, and an apple line. "We packed our own apples in 1961, 1962, and 1963, which Fruit Growers sold for us," he said. "We would pack them in the fall and hold them, hoping to sell in the spring when the price was higher."

Another Ranch Cold Storage Unit Under Construction In Wenatchee

BUILDING STEMILT GROWERS – A clipping from a newspaper article in 1960 about Tom building his first warehouse on Stemilt Hill.

Tom was relentless. In 1964, he bought cherry packing equipment and built a cherry packing building, creating a corporation called Stemilt Growers, Inc. "Stemilt's function was to do the packing and marketing of the fruit, and work on getting the best return back to the growers," he said.

It was working. "A buyer from New York City called me, and said he wanted to come out to see what we do to our cherries," Tom said. "He told me they shine like rubies and he couldn't believe how much better they were than anyone else's."

At just about the point that Tom felt Stemilt might be on the road to success, Mother Nature cut everyone down to size. In 1966, a huge cherry crop was hit by one of the hardest rains the area had seen. "Everybody thought the cherry season was over," Tom said. "The warehouses in Wenatchee all closed down."

YOUNG TREES – Tom tending to a newly planted tree atop Stemilt Hill in 1960.

But Tom saw something few others noticed. "All of the damage was out at the end of the limb," he noted. "I figured if we were careful with what we picked, we could sell the good ones. So that's what we did. I had to raise the price to $6.00 a box to pay for all the sorting, but we sold the whole crop."

It wasn't long before other growers took note, and asked if they could bring their cherries to Stemilt. "Paul Cammack asked if he could bring his cherries in," Tom remembered. "He sorted them and brought them in; we sorted them more and shipped them out. I took the check out to him and he thought there was a mistake. He returned more than he ever had in his life, and was literally moved to tears."

The packing shed at this time was run by family and neighbors, with Tom as the fieldman, packer, salesman, controlled atmosphere supervisor, quality control coordinator, and accountant at night. Stemilt was adding more growers at a rapid pace, including Gordon

Cammack, Ed Kane, Ralph Hedges, Ron Myers, and Chuck Atwood.

"I met Ron Cameron at about this time," Tom remembered. "He probably did more to help Stemilt over the years than anyone. He helped plan our expansion with ideas that always looked to the future."

Ron, an architect and engineer, worked with Tom for over 35 years, planning many building projects, ranging from small controlled atmosphere rooms on Stemilt Hill to the state-of-the-art facility at Olds Station. They had a love-hate relationship, and frequently argued over plans. "We would close his office door and yell at each other," Ron recalls.

HARD WORKER – Tom was a hard worker who put long hours in the orchard, warehouse and going over bookkeeping. This picture shows Tom hard at work in a pear orchard around 1960.

But Ron always respected Tom's passion for quality. "It didn't matter if it was a roof or a piece of fruit, quality was extremely important to Tom," Ron recalls. "We started building cold storage rooms and I was going to put a wood roof in the design, but Tom wanted a concrete roof which had never been done at the time. It was much more expensive, but Tom liked that it was quality and would give a better seal on the room."

Tom took some gut-wrenching chances during those years. After buying a new full-sized cherry line and taking in investment money from Gail Richardson, and Bill and Gene Chadderton, a market glut that year meant that prices were low. "We ended the season with a cold room full of packed cherries," Tom remembered. "People were saying we were broke and wouldn't be able to pay our growers."

Tom had faith in the packing methods he employed, though, and figured his fruit could hold out a

little longer than everyone else's because of it. He delayed shipping and was told by more than one expert that he was crazy. "The next week, the market price doubled and a few days later we were all shipped out!" he recalled. "Over the years, this scenario played itself out repeatedly."

BIRTHDAY AT THE WAREHOUSE – Tom celebrated many birthdays while at work and was often called out by employees for being late to his own party. This picture was taken at the Stemilt Hill warehouse in 1965.

Tom continued to invest in the company, buying property at Olds Station in 1972 to build his biggest facility yet. "I heard that Jam Food would sell six acres just north of the new bridge," Tom said. "The property was 330 feet wide and 1,110 feet long. I wrote a letter and offered them $60,000 cash for it."

With the deal consummated, Tom turned to Ron Cameron for advice. "He came by on a cold Friday afternoon and we discussed plans for the site for several hours," Tom remembered. "Finally, he threw the site plan on the floor and said, 'This is no good! Not enough room and too narrow!'"

Tom listened to Ron rant and rave for a while, and then said, "Well, it's what we have and we'll have to use it."

OLDS STATION 1986 – Construction began on the Olds Station facility in 1974. With the help of architect Ron Cameron, Tom designed and constructed a full-scale storing, packing and shipping facility, which became the hub of Stemilt's operations.

The next Monday, Tom received a site plan that worked, but it required purchasing another 20 acres of land to make it happen. Tom trusted in Ron's advice, moved forward on the project, and watched the Olds plant prove its worth many times over in the years ahead.

In 1979, Tom moved his office to the Olds plant and, for the first time in his career, had to drive to work. "I would check the Hill plant, get the mail at the post office, work in the warehouse or office all day, and get home for supper at night," he remembered. "Stemilt was taking on more growers and building more CA storages. Things were really coming together."

With quality packing facilities, Tom wanted to ensure a long supply of fruit. So he encouraged growers from lower altitudes on Stemilt Hill to bring their fruit to him. "A lot of growers objected to the idea, thinking it would be fruit of old varieties and the end of our market," he said, "but I knew we had to have more volume if we were going to have market presence."

It was a major decision that helped Stemilt grow. Later, the company invested in orchards in California and Tom's son, Kyle, expanded his operations to Chile, all with the sole purpose of keeping the supply coming for as long as possible. If Stemilt could provide retailers with an uninterrupted supply of quality product, the company could hold a leadership position.

Tom also had the foresight to develop partnerships that would last for decades, to the advantage of all parties. A great example is the Lucky Badger Ranch north of Orondo, Washington. Planted in 1965, it was offered for sale as 62 individual 10-acre blocks. Each block had a different parcel number and a specific owner, mostly U.S. Army officers who had been helicopter pilots in Vietnam. Having escaped the war, they decided to stick together by jointly investing in an orchard, even though they lived in different parts of the country. Things went fine until the 1980's when the changing marketplace was making production loans hard to get and interest rates soar. Few apple growers could even qualify for a production loan and those who did couldn't afford to pay the interest rates.

"Lucky Badger was without operating financing for the coming season and the creditors were pushing forward to foreclosure," recalls Dave Mathison, Tom's nephew and grower. "The orchard was already in tough shape due to dwindling funds. Trees had not been hand pruned for years and at least 30% of the trees had extensive mouse and winter damage."

Filing for bankruptcy to protect their assets, Lucky Badger, Inc. and its growers turned to Stemilt for help preparing a recovery plan to present to the creditors and bankruptcy judge. "We prepared a five-year business plan that would pay off the creditors," Dave says. "None of the creditors had much faith in the apple industry or the ranch, and most would not support the plan, wanting the judge to sell the property."

The judge, however, believed in Tom's vision and Stemilt's recovery plan with strict monthly reporting to all parties. He approved moving forward with it.

That was only the first step. "None of the local commercial banks would loan Stemilt the operating financing for the ranch, not even Stemilt's primary lender," Dave says. "They told Tom he would be wise to stay away from the project, but Tom saw the potential of the well-laid out orchard and varieties, and he believed Stemilt could operate the ranch with enough margin to pay off the creditors."

One bank finally agreed to loan Tom the money, with a guarantee from Stemilt that, if the crop revenue was insufficient to repay the loan, the company would still pay up.

Under Tom's careful stewardship, Lucky Badger returned to its prime capabilities in a shockingly short time, and the creditors were paid off, with interest, a full year ahead of schedule, returning the land back to the owners debt free. "All of the grower block owners were so pleased, they signed a 10-year agreement with Stemilt to continue managing their orchards," Dave says. "Now, years later, after 29 wind machines, eight family homes for permanent employees, facilities for 100 guest harvest workers, a new fleet of tractors and sprayers, and literally millions of dollars paid out to the Lucky Badger growers, Stemilt continues managing the ranch."

AERIAL – Lucky Badger Orchards spreads out across the landscape.

Dave remembers Tom's firebrand style of passion for Lucky Badger's success. "We would drive up to the ranch in Tom's El Camino, park it, and he would take off hiking," Dave says. "He could look at an orchard and hike at about eight miles per hour at the same time. I could tell when he didn't like how something was pruned or if he saw too many bruises in a bin, but he would keep on moving. It was my job to stop and work with the crew to get them to do the job right."

With 620 acres of land to roam, Dave lost Tom frequently. "Sometimes we'd not be able to find the car," he recalls. "Sometimes we'd find each other before we found the car and no one would say a word about it. When I found the car first, I would always wait for him. I'm sure he often waited for me as well, but I can tell you, I had to hitchhike back to town by myself a few times!"

Tom continued to innovate, turning some of the blocks to organic farming as he was convinced it was the way of the future. "One of the growers was so upset with the change, he flew from his home in southern California to have a private meeting with Tom to demand to know why we were turning his block into organic without consulting him," Dave remembers. "He insisted that Stemilt make up any shortfall in revenue that he might face from our organic farming practices."

Dave laughs. "We should have negotiated to share in the ups if returns were better than conventional methods, but we didn't," he recalls. "On the second or third organic crop, we sent him a check for his net profit on one 10-acre block that was about $180,000. He called and said there must be some kind of mistake on his check and he wanted to make sure it was real before he cashed it!"

The willingness to adapt, to change, and to grow was the hallmark of Tom's success. He was never too young to try something out; he was never too old to learn something new. Life was one big learning experience, and Tom's passion for excellence kept him always moving forward.

Chapter 8

Working for TK

Bob Mathison, Tom's eldest son, thinks of his Dad as two different people—Daddy and TK.

Daddy was warm, funny, affectionate, and steady as a rock.

TK was an altogether different person. TK was the boss and he held everyone who worked for him to the same high standard he expected from himself, a standard that was often very difficult to achieve.

"TK was full of gumption," Bob remembers, "and I always wondered why the hired men liked him so much."

One of those reasons might have been that people sensed Tom's loyalty and his respect for them

AT THE OFFICE – Tom kept a steady routine of long work hours, but always made time to pick up the mail on his way to work and personally deliver paychecks to his employees.

and their contributions. Ron Cameron remembers advising Tom at one point to make some changes on the lines to tighten up expenses, some of which included firing people. "Tom said that was not an option," Ron recalls. "We did make some changes that helped lessen costs, but kept the people,

PACKING INNOVATIONS – From Stemilt-branded PLU stickers to being the first to pack cherries in bags, Tom made sure Stemilt was at the forefront of innovation. Here, he examines a new cherry bagger with Darcey Brown and Steve Hisel in 2003.

because that was extremely important to Tom."

Bob found that being the eldest son had few privileges. "I started working when I was six years old, changing sprinklers in the summer," he says. "I remember being in Grandma's yard one hot day, getting a drink of water out of a drinking fountain that she had put up for us kids. TK drove up and told me to quit wasting water by drinking it! I guess he thought the water was more important for the trees than for me."

As he got older, Bob worked with George Bainard changing sprinklers, while Kyle was partnered with Charlie Krantz. "As kids, we were always messing up, but George and Charlie would help us fix whatever we did," Bob says. "TK, though, would go with us on Saturdays and Sundays. When he was there, we would catch holy hell when we messed up! Back then, we had two-inch, 20-ft. long aluminum sprinkler pipe that we moved from row-to-row and block-to-block. The problem was the blocks weren't square. If you needed more pipe to catch the corner trees, you had to find some and put them on. If you forgot, the corner tree didn't get water. Believe me, if you forgot and TK found out, that's when it hit the fan!"

Bob seemed to have a special talent for messing up with a forklift. "It seemed I was always hitting something," he laughs. "One time, I hit a wet spot in front of the pop machine and drove the forklift right through the wall. Bill Bainard was in charge of the warehouse and he just calmly told me to get that fixed before your old man sees it."

Bob worked furiously through his break until almost quitting time, finding a few old 2 x 4's, patching them in, and hanging a "No Smoking" sign over the repair to hide it. "I don't think TK ever noticed," he says.

He wasn't so lucky the next time. "I was high-piling collapsible bins with the forklift when I just nudged a bin on the side as I was backing out," he recalls. "All of a sudden, the bottom bin collapsed and two stacks of towering fruit fell, missing me by inches! The fruit ran out the door and across the slab, almost making it to the county road."

THE MATHISON FAMILY – Tom, Lorraine, and the extended Mathison family pose for a family picture in 2003.

Of course, who should come around the corner at just that moment, but TK?

"There was a moment of deafening silence," Bob says, "Then, TK looked at me and just said, 'I think it would be better if you worked in the orchard.'"

Luckily for Bob, orchard work was a natural, though his methods were sometimes different from Tom's. "TK would tell me his philosophy was to farm each tree separately," Bob remembers. "Each tree should be fertilized as an individual, and not range managed. I tried to use his philosophy, but later as I got more orchards, I realized I was doing what he said not to, and I still range manage orchards."

Bob and Kyle met Tom every Saturday morning at 8:30 sharp to drive through each orchard on the hill and discuss what they were doing wrong. "Kyle and TK usually got into an argument about something which made me the referee," Bob says.

Bob learned, too, that TK would not abide shortcuts. "I learned what TK liked to see and made sure that it was up to

CHERRY KING – Following in his father's footsteps, Kyle was named Cherry King in 2008. Tom received the honor in 1971. Tom is pictured here with Kyle, his grandsons Tate and West, and great-grandsons, Finn and Jax.

snuff," he recalls. "If I didn't agree with him, I learned to prune the trees that he looked at his way, and then do the rest of the block my way."

That worked out fine until TK got a 4-wheeler. "Then he sure caught on and I told him it was the 4-wheeler's fault," Bob laughs. "I had to do things his way after that."

When TK moved on to his own orchards and spent less time critiquing Bob's, Bob says he oddly missed it. "I felt that if TK said it was O.K., then it was O.K.," he notes. "Now I wasn't sure if I was farming correctly."

Tom had a knack for cutting right to the chase, or the truth of the matter, in his dealings with people. One large grower demanded a reduced handling charge from Stemilt, pointing out that his bins were smaller than the ones Stemilt used, and other warehouses were giving him a discount. Tom quickly replied that it cost just as much to move the smaller bins as it did the larger ones and, if there was going to be an adjusted price, then Stemilt should be charging him more. After a moment of shock, the grower smiled, shook Tom's hand, and ended up bringing a major portion of his fruit to Stemilt for many years.

An early-season cherry grower with a maverick reputation sat down for an introductory meeting with Tom and was taken aback when Tom's first words were, "I understand you're a little hard to get along with." He retorted, "Tom, I understand you're the same way!" The two laughed, got the truth of the matter out on the table, and proceeded to hammer out a deal.

Dave Mathison remembers over-thinning an orchard, and then following Tom as he reviewed it, trying to keep up with Tom's speedy gait, and dreading his sure-to-come opinion. Apples were dropping off limbs right and left, covering the ground, when Dave suggested it was perhaps the most successful thinning job he had ever done. "Looks to me like you passed successful about three days ago," Tom replied.

Another time, Dave asked Tom to drive through a distressed orchard that the owners had hoped Stemilt could turn around. "Tom always drove, so he could look at the good spots, as well as the bad," says Dave, "and he had an instinct to be able to drive right up to the driest, worst tree on any ranch."

For what seemed like an eternity, Tom drove in complete silence. Finally, he turned to Dave and said, "Congratulations. If you were trying to find the worst

MATHISON MEN – Three generations of Mathisons on a 1923 Model T orchard truck in 2008.

orchard in the state of Washington, I think you found it." Even so, he developed a business plan with the owners, provided encouragement to those working on it, and, in a few years, the ranch was in tip-top shape.

In 1992, the banks started to talk Tom about leadership succession of the family business. Tom had a strong sense that a blood relative should take over, but having watched many family farming operations struggle during transitions, he didn't like the discussion. Besides the strain of picking the right leader, the worry of being fair to everyone in the family, and his concern with employee response to the change, he also wondered what he would do each day. How was he supposed to go from working 12-14 hours a day, making all major decisions, to slowing down? He understood the need and the reasons, but the idea of not having a job to do began to haunt him. There were a few family business meetings where the topic of succession was discussed. Tom would stew and not say much as ideas and concepts were bounced around. Finally, he would announce to the room that he was done discussing the subject and he was ready to move on to items of more importance.

"Over the years, Tom would discuss different ideas with his attorney, Peter Spadoni, and select family members," says Tom's grandson, West. "Prior to 1992, Tom would say with some sarcasm that, upon his death, he expected it to be a dog fight with the strongest one getting the most. I think these remarks were repeated and found their way to his bankers. Wisely, Tom knew he needed to start a real discussion."

One of the recommendations was to have a formal board of directors which could provide insight and discussion around succession. Several people were recommended and a list of directors was selected. The slate was impressive, and included Jim Ware, an HR consultant from the IEC Group, Ron Meyers, a grower and former mayor of Wenatchee, Barry Thomas with Russell Investments, and Bill Douglas, president of Douglas Fruit Company. The outside directors were a good influence on Tom. They were able to scope out the size and magnitude of the task ahead. Tom's son-in-law, Hans van Someren Gréve, who worked for a large international manufacturing company, was asked to join the board along with Kyle, Bob, and Dave.

Up until 1992, the active family members were all engaged in the growing side of the business and did not have much experience in the storage, packing, and selling

FAMILY BUSINESS – As Stemilt expanded, Tom's sons and relatives became more involved in the company and it truly became a family business. This picture was taken of the Mathison men at the Cherry Roundup BBQ held in 1990.

part. Hans added value by flying in from Europe and Japan to contribute to the board meetings. He provided a good perspective with his rich experience of international markets. Kyle, Bob, and Dave were able to take more active roles outside of the farming end.

In spring of 1996, Tom started the succession process by announcing his intentions at a staff meeting. He discussed, in an awkward manner, the fact that he wanted to start down a path that might lead to retirement…some day. He laid out his plan that would divide the operations of Stemilt into two roles. Bob would lead Production, Operations, and Quality Control. Kyle would oversee Sales, Marketing, Human Resources, and Research and Development. The idea seemed logical, but there were concerns with the lack of experience both sons had in these new roles. Both Bob and Kyle worked to learn the business and establish relationships with their new direct reports, but many of the directors still saw Tom as their boss and Tom continued to give them direction. Kyle and Tom were passionate about the business, but had very different approaches. There were a number of occasions when emotions ran high and hot. Everyone's intentions were genuine, but the plan was not working well.

In the summer of 1997, opportunity and timing would coincide as Hans left the company he was working for in Germany to join Stemilt as General Manager. This was a proud event for Tom. He had always dreamed of running his business with his sons, son-in-law, and nephew—one big happy family. The move brought Lavonne home to Wenatchee with her two children, Lillian and Stephen. Having all of their children and grandchildren living in Wenatchee was very special to Tom and Lorraine.

Tom and Hans reorganized the company. With Hans' background in marketing and manufacturing, he assumed the leadership of Sales, Marketing, Production, and Operations. Kyle had a passion for people and innovation, and continued with Human Resources and Research and Development. Bob's personal relationship skills and farming experience made him a good fit to run the field staff and Quality Control. Tom maintained the Finance and Accounting group led by Dan Rothrock. Tom and Dan were very close and worked well together.

Stemilt grew at a fast pace. Dave was growing the Stemilt Management farming company, while Tom and Hans worked to build storage and packing facilities to handle the growth. Stemilt also ventured into the

A CHANGING INDUSTRY– With his pioneering spirit, Tom led the adoption of many new varieties in order to prepare Stemilt for the future growth. Pictured here are: Bob, Kyle, Tom, and Hans.

marketing services business by consolidating the sales force of Peshastian Hi-Up Grower's Cooperative and Orondo Fruit.

"In addition, the family had to pull together during a Teamsters Union campaign, and the challenges of battling the union were difficult," West recalls. "Tom did a radio interview on local station KPQ. You could tell in his voice he had passion for his employees and wanted to do what he could, not to have a wedge driven between him and his employees. After four years, the employees of Stemilt decided they did not want the union and the family was greatly relieved."

During these years, West worked for Stemilt during the summer months, doing various jobs in Human Resources, Production, and Sales. After graduating from college, he worked outside the business in consulting and grocery before returning in 2002. Tom and West worked very well together. Kyle said he could see how it was easier for Tom to work with his grandson than his son. This scenario had repeated itself, as Kyle had taken over the operations of the orchards from his grandmother. Tom felt a sense of purpose in mentoring West, and, in return, West admired and appreciated his grandfather, and highly valued his input.

West worked on special projects in many areas of Stemilt until Tom decided to promote him to Executive Vice President in the winter of 2003. Then, in June 2005, on Tom's 79th birthday, he relinquished the role of President to West. In a birthday party in the conference room, Tom, with confidence and pride, announced West's promotion and described his new role. Tom wanted to continue picking up the mail, taking payroll around, and farming his personal orchards which totaled 850 acres.

During a produce convention, Tom had a conversation with the patriarch and founder of a large family-owned vegetable company who was disappointed in his own succession plan. This conversation would stick with him. Tom quoted the patriarch: "In a family business, someone has to be in charge. Having a bunch of family members working together with equal say and influence eventually leads to infighting and disaster. The buck has got to stop with someone."

Before Tom's passing, many of his grandchildren were working in the business, a fact that gave him much pride. Kyle's younger son, Tate, returned home to work in Sales after working four years for Dole Produce in Los Angeles. Also, Tom was very proud of the accomplishments of Bob's son, Aaron, and Dave's sons, Curtis and Noel. He would say with a large grin and passion, "I love the ambition I see in these kids."

Kyle, says one thing was a constant with TK—he was always fair in his dealings with people. "But I think the trait I admired most was the way he developed trust with the growers, the employees, and the customer," Kyle says. "He would say that Stemilt on the box was his promise. The growers and employees trusted him to do the right thing."

Kyle also remembers TK's joy in sharing the results of hard work. "He loved to take out the payroll and give the checks to employees personally, shaking every guy's hand and saying, 'Thank you for your help and your contribution,'" he recalls. "He took a long time to do that. Looking back, I can see where it was really worth it."

Tom also loved to personally handle the mail bag and the bank deposit bag. "He loved to see the money roll in and see his baby Stemilt prosper and grow," Kyle says. "He would take in a deposit and come back with an apple box full of letters. He felt proud of this tangible evidence that his 'baby' was growing and was going to make it in this world."

Kyle thinks this pride may very well be a family legacy. "I remember my Grandma, AJ, the boss lady," he says. "When I was six years old, just coming out of first grade, I was changing sprinklers and she told me, 'Listen, Kyle, you're no longer going to call me Grandma. I'm

A SHARED PASSION – Kyle, West, and Tom together in a cherry orchard, always striving to produce the very best fruit.

AJ and your Dad is TK. We're in business together now. You're a Mathison.'"

Tom loved to be out in the orchards more than anything, and anyone who worked with him knew that. It brought him pleasure in every stage of his life. "In later years, he would help me on the cherry orchard in Chile," Kyle says. "There were a lot of dead trees that had to come out, so we rented a pickup and we would pull them."

Kyle smiles when he remembers. "I would hook a chain around the tree and say, 'hit it!' Then TK would pop the clutch and snap the slack out of the chain," Kyle laughs. "The trees would pop right out of the ground. TK said, 'I bet when they rented you this pickup, they didn't figure it was going to be used as a bulldozer!' We had a lot of fun."

Chapter 9

Tom-isms

Tom had certain phrases that he would use regularly that more or less summed up some of his strongest beliefs and core values. These are a few:

QUALITY FIRST – Tom made many visits to the warehouse to inspect fruit quality or interact with employees.

Honesty is the best policy. He believed in building relationships around trust and respect, and those relationships would last for years. He treated customers, vendors, employees, and contractors as valued, trusted partners. "Confidence and trust are earned," he would say, "never granted."

Do it right the first time. Tom firmly believed it was the only way to do things. "You always did the right thing even it if cost more," Steve Shiflett, close friend, grower, and retired employee, remembered. "He would tell me that I had to use it over and over or drive over it for a very long time, so the first time was the best time to get it right."

A clean house is a happy house. "Tom always told me that people would work better if we kept our house in order," Shiflett says. "Clean floors, no black

SELLING CHERRIES – Over the years, Tom frequently visited customers to not only sell his fruit, but build lasting relationships. This picture is of Tom and Steve Shiflett on a business trip in the late 1970's.

marks, etc. I would take pride in doing the monthly warehouse inspections because I think this helps make Stemilt a good place to work."

This is a business of faith. "Some people have it and some don't," says Mike Taylor, VP of Sales & Marketing. "Tom would tell me you have to be able to walk out into a dormant orchard and just believe."

It's about selling a program and a culture, not about selling a load. "The absolute most incredible thing was to watch Tom in front of a Stemilt customer," Taylor recalls. "There would be a sparkle in his eye, and he'd be full of passion, pride, and natural charisma. Tom was the definition of authentic!"

Nothing sells the product like the product itself. Tom believed the customer was the judge and jury. "Let them vote with their dollars," he would say. He felt that cherries tended to be an impulse item, and his job was making them the very best they could be, so that customers couldn't help but pick them up.

PASSION FOR THE FIELD – The orchard was perhaps Tom's favorite place of all to be. He loved going on drives through the blocks to see the fruit progress through the seasons.

Hire the best people. Teach and empower them. "Tom said the best thing you could do was let great people lift you up and make you better," Taylor says. Most importantly, Tom would say, "Never ask your employees to do anything you won't do yourself."

People's perception is their reality. "Tom always took the opportunity to use life events as a way to lead, inspire, and teach people," Taylor says. "Building people up was a natural and regular practice for Tom. He did it through his wisdom and enthusiasm. He really made you believe in yourself and in your team. As a direct result, the people around Tom were able to reach heights and accomplish things beyond their own expectations."

Success builds success. Tom thought it was important to recognize success in others, and to do everything he could to help people around him build self-confidence. "When people accomplish something and they're successful at it and they recognize why, well then, they want to repeat that situation in their lives," he said.

THE NEXT GENERATION – Tom transferred the Stemilt presidency to his grandson West Mathison in 2005. Though technically retired, Tom was still very involved in Stemilt until his passing in 2008.

There are three kinds of people in this world—smart people, shrewd people, and wise people. "Some people are lucky enough to have more than one of these gifts," Tom said.

When asked which gift he believed he had, he didn't hesitate to answer.

"I know I'm not smart," he said, "and I'm not shrewd. So that leaves me to be wise, to have judgment. I decided I was wise enough to be able to tell when people had good ideas about what would work and what wouldn't work. And I had enough humility to accept what they said, give them credit for it, and adopt it."

If I did everything the bank recommended I do, I'd still be farming 40 acres on Stemilt Hill. Dave Mathison, Tom's nephew, says he heard this statement from Tom every time the company was about to embark on something risky, something that might make others hesitate. "I think it was his way to inspire us to a level of urgency," Dave says, "and to give the matter all the attention we could. It was up to us to make sure the result was successful."

THE BIG 79 – Tom at his 79th birthday party, held at the office, on June 23, 2005.

If you don't care, they don't care. "TK cared about the employees and their families," says son Kyle. "He wanted the best for them—health insurance, 401(k)'s. In return, the employees cared about Stemilt. TK cared about quality and consistency in every box we shipped. He cared about the retailers, and wanted to be sure we were servicing them well."

For TK, caring was the bottom line, and was the one thing that mattered the most.

It's by the absolute grace of God that we are born into this country, in these times, and in this industry. Tom felt we had an obligation to go out and see what we could make with all of our opportunities and advantages.

Chapter 10

We Remember

I received a phone call early one spring morning telling me that Tom Mathison wanted to meet with me later that morning. Being the school principal, my first thought was, "Oh no, what was wrong?"

I hurried to check in with the various teachers who had Tom's grandkids in their classes to see whether they had any idea why Tom wanted to meet with me. No one had a clue. They assured me that all was going well. I had no idea what was to happen at that meeting, and how it was to impact Mission View Elementary School for many years to come.

Sure enough, Tom sat down in my office that sunny morning and shared a story. He said on his way down the hill, he had passed a group of his employee's children waiting for the school bus. At that very moment, he felt that God was charging him with the responsibility for making their lives and their schooling as positive as possible. So TK asked me, "How can we, meaning Stemilt Growers and the Mathison family, help?"

Boy, let me tell you, an offer of assistance like that doesn't happen every day in the life of a rural elementary school principal! We talked in general terms about how he might help and then set a meeting for later that spring to continue our discussions. That initial meeting was the groundwork for our relationship with Stemilt and Tom's involvement with his favorite programs at Mission View.

At our next meeting in TK's office, we set up a game plan. It was obvious that our student population was shifting and we needed more help connecting with our Spanish-speaking families and their children. We devised a way for Stemilt to fund a half-time Spanish paraeducator to work with this home-to-school connection. The beauty of this program was it came with no strings attached. We could use the program as we saw fit.

During the years, we accomplished some pretty incredible things. We were able to start a Mexican folk dance troupe that performed all over the state. We hosted an annual holiday dinner party for our families and staff, complete with TK and Lorraine carving and serving the turkey. I believe, at one time or another, we must have had almost all of the Mathison clan in the kitchen at Mission View working on this wonderful event!

Another of the unbelievable connections Tom helped us with was the "use" of Steve Shiflett, Stemilt's general construction supervisor. Tom gave me the green light to use Steve for any and all Mission View projects. The students and school community benefited in so many ways. Our ugly bank facing the river was landscaped, irrigated, and maintained by Stemilt. Our new outdoor basketball court on the playground was a dream—their sturdy backboard supports looked surprisingly like leftover irrigation pipe to me and worked great!

One year on carnival day, we just didn't have enough parent help to get the carnival set up. One call to Kyle Mathison, Tom's son, and his wife, Jan, was all it took. Within an hour, I had at least 10 strong helpers and two flatbed trucks at my disposal.

TK made it clear from the beginning that these gifts of time and talent were to be strictly between him and me. He definitely didn't want his help to be publicized or for him to be honored for it in any way.

That was Tom Mathison's way—diligently working to make the world a better place in any way he knew how, quietly and behind the scenes.

Joe St. Jean
Principal
Mission View Elementary School

Friend! Yes, we have been friends for many years, since we were in the 5th grade at South Wenatchee School.

You, my brother Tom, Helen, and I had many good times together, especially coasting parties on the hill. Tom and I would bring our team of horses with a bobsled and pull the coasters back up the hill. Then we would put our team in your barn, stay overnight, and go home the next day.

Do you remember how Ernie Steffen let us get off the bus on Stemilt Creek bridge? We didn't have to ride that long way up to the Cammack's and Knouf's. I have pictures of a few stops we made. Good times!

My father also considered your Dad the most special and good man on Stemilt Hill. He loved visiting with him and their thoughts and ambitions were almost alike.

My sons, Jeff and Dane, admire you more than anyone else I can think of. We are all proud of the great success you have become. It speaks well for our type of upbringing—to work hard, take advantage of opportunities, and not be afraid to gamble with your dreams. TK, I salute you!

I always was glad to see you at Grange and hear you call me "Mini Lou." You are the only one who remembered my nickname and it always made me feel glad and well-liked.

All I can say is it has been a great privilege to call you friend.

Mini Lou Keene

When I think of Grandpa, I instantly think of his cologne that seemed to linger after each hug. He also liked to chew Wrigley's double-mint gum. The scents would combine and become a source of comfort and nostalgia for me.

When we stayed over at Grandpa and Grandma's, we would always have a piece of gum after dinner. He had his stash of gum in the same place—in the cupboard over the stove, bottom right-hand corner, right next to the steak cutters.

He had a pretty good sense of humor with us kids. I remember how he would notice if we weren't cleaning our plates. He would smile ever so sweetly, lean over, and say in a kind voice, "Would you like for me to help you? You seem to have trouble eating today." Somehow, the food would be eaten and we would go on to have our piece of gum.

I will always associate him with being a morning person. We grandkids (sometimes just Aaron, my brother, and I, and sometimes all of the cousins) would spend the night and, no matter if it were the weekend or a school day, we would get up bright and early in the morning. "Got no time to be lollygagging around," Grandpa would say. "It's time to start a new day. Grandma's got a nice hot breakfast going and we have things to do!"

He was always on the move, reading the news and keeping up with current events. I never saw him get overwhelmed about anything to the point of quitting. Sure, he would get mad, but he put that energy into fixing the problem. If anything, you would get an eye-roll and an "Oh, brother!", but he would keep going until everything was right once more.

I remember sitting at the table together, talking, when someone mentioned that we might be related to Donald Trump. Grandpa sat there for a moment, and then said, quite casually, "Well, good for him!"

He never was one to be star-struck or jealous of anyone else's achievements. He had a good sense of who he was and what he could do. No one could convince him that any one of us could ever get away with just using the bare minimum of our talents.

Joyce Mathison
Tom's granddaughter

I first met Tom over 20 years ago when I was in Michigan working for Meijer. He would make trips to see all his good customers with a Stemilt staff member or two at his side. Tom would want to know everything about his product, such as the quality on arrival, how it was selling, where it was displayed, how it was advertised, what the price points were going to be in future weeks, and so much more. He would ask to go to the warehouse to examine his products. He would often take gas samples of modified atmosphere bags that held his cherries with a device he brought with him. I marveled at his enthusiasm as well as his pride in what he did.

As a young (at the time) retailer, I felt special that an icon such as he was in our produce industry would take the time to come to see me. Although I always felt in awe of his fame, I did feel that Tom had the same enthusiasm and passion about our colorful industry as

I did. Tom knew that our real boss was that consumer pushing the shopping cart.

When I began my career at Stemilt as Marketing Director, I realized that Tom's passion had no boundaries. Tom and I traveled together many times. We visited customers and trade events together. Tom knew how to sell his company through his passion. He would share his new ideas with the customers and also share his personal life back in Wenatchee with the people he enjoyed. Tom was so proud of his children and wife and would boast of their accomplishments. He also bragged about his grandchildren and frequently told stories about them. I learned so much from his stories and knowledge of the fruit business.

He loved visiting retailers and wholesale customers. He knew the airports well and had the drill down. Upon arriving at our destination, I would have a car reserved. Tom loved to drive, especially to new destinations that he hadn't explored. He would ask "Do you want to drive?" I would always tell him that I was tired and would he mind taking the driving duties? This of course was exactly what he wanted to hear. He would say, "I'll drive and you navigate off the map."

He also took great pleasure in anticipating what car we would have waiting. I knew to look for a deal when renting a car in advance, but yet not disappoint him. Once we went to Toronto together and had the smallest Kia ever made (one of the early models). He looked at me with scorn and said "What the heck is this?" In a panicked response, I shouted back, "A Korean Cadillac!" We jumped in and he drove into the jumbled traffic of Toronto, and he was just fine with it.

When traveling, Tom would look forward to stopping at every retail store possible (and I do mean every one!). He also loved a great meal out. He would spar with servers when the service was poor, and when he felt the prices were high, he'd say, "You are awfully proud of your steaks!" He once made me laugh so hard in Chicago when he told a waitress, "These are the worst rolls I have ever had in my entire life!" She was grumpy and deserved his disapproval. They argued with each other all dinner long and Tom, of course, got the final word when it came time to tip.

I always had the greatest respect for Tom as a boss and he always treated me well. He never once raised his voice with me, even when we disagreed. It helped that we often thought alike, but I also realized that we had a special relationship that was almost like family. He would always stop and visit in the morning when in the office. He would ask first about Joni and Alex, my wife and son, then he would talk about travel and gardening, two passions we shared, and, last, he would ask about customers and what programs we were working on.

I will always remember Tom's futuristic vision in the business, his respect and concern for the consumer, and his love for family and friends. There will never be anyone quite like him.

Roger Pepperl
Marketing Director
Stemilt Growers, Inc.

From 1980 until 1988, I was the orchard manager for Mack Richey's Sumac Orchards near the airport in East Wenatchee, WA. He is my brother-in-law and his wife is my older sister. The orchards were an investment financed through his primary occupation as a plastic surgeon in Seattle.

For six of the eight years that I worked for Mack, we enjoyed a good working relationship which I attribute primarily to the fact that I am a tolerant person and he only came to Wenatchee for a day every week or so. Mack can be a very difficult person to work with because he believes that his opinion is always the correct one and his knowledge is superior to that of others, regardless of what the topic of conversation might be.

After a rather contentious final two years, Mack decided to try to save money by having his orchards managed by Stemilt Management. He had always been impressed by the Mathison family, and he believed his growing costs would be substantially reduced because he would be able to take advantage of Stemilt Management's economy of scale in labor, materials, and chemicals. I was released from my position and moved on to perform quality control inspections for a California export company for two years before becoming an export fruit salesperson.

In 1993, I was invited to participate in a trade mission to China by the Washington Apple Commission. Among those in the delegation was Tom Mathison, representing Stemilt Growers, Inc. I had been only cordially acquainted with Tom over the years due to the proximity of Sumac Orchards to orchards that Tom's company either owned or managed. During our tour of China, I took advantage of several opportunities to sit next to Tom during flights, bus rides, and meals to become friends and better know this icon of the fruit business.

During a bus ride to Shanghai, curiosity got the best of me and I turned to Tom and asked, "So, Tom, how are you getting along with Mack Richey?"

After several long minutes without an answer, I was about to rephrase the question, thinking that perhaps he had not heard me the first time.

Just then, Tom turned to me and answered in his signature wise and gravelly voice, "I sure do appreciate Mack taking valuable time away from his plastic surgery business every week to come teach me how to grow apples."

Rich Roberts
Former Import and Procurement Manager
Stemilt Growers, Inc.

I started working in the Stemilt office at Olds Station back in the late 1980's. Kari Racus and I shared an office. Tom would come in to say hello and find out what you were working on. Whether you were sitting at your desk or not, he would look through the paperwork on your desk. If he saw something that wasn't familiar to him, he would ask about it and sometimes take it with him.

We'd been told that Tom looked through all the mail before it was distributed. I would sometimes receive an envelope that had already been opened, so I believe this was true. Tom seemed to know everything that was happening. I was amazed at how he could keep his thumb on everything and know everybody.

I was told that, if Tom ever called in and asked what you were doing, never say, "oh, nothing." Rumor had it that a receptionist once said this to him and he became very upset and demanded to know why he was paying her to do nothing!

But Tom always made sure we knew he appreciated us. I will never forget how special he made me feel.

Lisa Mitchell
Business Support Analyst
Stemilt Growers, Inc.

I first met Tom in 1970 when I came down from Brewster to rent collapsible bins. While waiting, I listened to him dealing with a cherry grower over charges. His firm, open, and direct manner made a profound impression on me, a young warehouse manager.

After moving to Wenatchee in 1972, I leased a small cherry orchard above the cemetery and became a Stemilt grower for several years. Tom mentored me, providing special help through some tough years of rain damage. I was treated royally, even though I was a grower of little significance, and I have never forgotten that. I recognized then that Stemilt's service to its growers was as good as it gets.

One year Stemilt absorbed a sizeable loss on Bartlett pears that should have been passed on to its growers, but Tom chose otherwise (an unusual occurrence in this industry). Tom had that pioneer drive to tackle a problem and do what he believed was right. My thought then was that this guy is a real leader, strong, honorable, and smart as hell. Tom proved to be that many times over the years.

He has been recognized as the Washington fruit industry's foremost visionary in the past half century. He was far ahead in recognizing the need for a change, and was bold and decisive in implementing his ideas, as well as providing leadership in tackling critical industry problems.

Tom was the first to see the value of directly servicing the retail trade. He struck out on his own and developed the trend that exists today.

Challenging the Washington Apple Commission's authority and dominance was his most notable undertaking. His willingness to break with tradition was unprecedented. He was soundly in the minority, but time has proven him right. After the Commission's restructuring, the ensuing competition among shippers has made them all better and more profitable, just as Tom predicted.

Tom lived life as an ordinary man, but his spirit led him to do extraordinary things. His efforts in building Stemilt into a formidable company has allowed the rest of the industry to benefit by riding on his coattails. We all owe him a debt of gratitude. He has given more than he ever received and his contributions have made our lives a lot better.

Bob Riggan
President
Gwin, White, & Prince

I began my career in the industry as a cherry sorter on Stemilt Hill. I was working summers and nights while I went to Wenatchee Valley College and Central Washington University. As Stemilt grew, I grew. Tom gave me an opportunity I believe I would never have received if I worked somewhere else.

I was given responsibility for production lines, production plants, then developing a quality control program with Sales. From there, I was given the opportunity to work closer to the customer base, traveling throughout the United States and the world.

Over time, my responsibilities would change, but there was always one constant. Every morning, Tom would stop by or call to say hello and see what was going on. I could tell stories about my travels with Tom, riding a car through the orchards, flying throughout the world, but I'd like to share something more personal because I believe it shows how much Tom cared for the employees of Stemilt, and that we were truly part of his family.

He told me that one of the toughest days of his life was when his mother died. He told me this because he knew I was close to my mom.

In May of 2008, I was talking to Tom on the cherry line at Chinchiolo Stemilt California. He told me he wasn't feeling well, and he was having trouble with his arm. Several weeks later, he came into my office and told me that he had cancer, and he was going to have to go through treatments to minimize the tumor before surgery. We talked about family and he wanted to know about my parents.

In August of that year, I walked into his office to share that my mother had been diagnosed with cancer, and that time was precious. She was not going to go through chemo or radiation, mainly because she didn't want to, but also because her health was so fragile. We were going to begin hospice care. He then told me he had surgery scheduled for September to remove the tumor. Every day up to his surgery, we talked at the office or on the phone. He wanted to know how I was doing with my mom, and he would explain what was going on with him.

On Sept. 11, I called his cell phone and told him my mom had passed away the previous evening. About two weeks later, I sat in Tom's office with Lorraine. He explained to me that his cancer had progressed. It was apparent that time was precious for Tom, too.

The Tom Mathison I knew was a man of integrity, vision, honesty, and passion. He was my employer, my mentor, and, most importantly, my best friend. Not a day goes by that I don't think of him.

Eva Lauve
Production Planning and Scheduling Manager
Stemilt Growers, Inc.

Tom taught me how to persevere in the face of rejection. In the early 1990's, my small company in Milton-Freewater, JDI Fruit, needed a better sales force. We thought we could entice Stemilt to sell our fruit. Though Tom expressed interest, he believed that all fruit Stemilt sells should be brought to Wenatchee. Rejection number one.

Shortly thereafter, we sold the company and I moved to Wenatchee to work for Dole Northwest. In 2001, Dole shut down its Wenatchee operation and I needed a job. I went to see Tom. In those days, the industry was in a significant downturn. Tom was concerned about his own company and how it was going to turn things around. "Sorry," he told me, "but we aren't hiring anybody right now." Rejection number two.

I eventually found a great job at Sagemoor Farms. Over the years there, a couple of opportunities came up to perhaps work for Stemilt. At one time, I would have taken one of those jobs because it was a new challenge, but I was turned down. Rejection number three.

One might think that, after all those rejections. I might have lost any interest in ever doing any business with Stemilt, but far from it. I have never lost my admiration for a great company, and the family and employees who built it.

Over the last 20 years, a good friend of mine, Dennis Courtier, and I have spent a great deal of time talking about apple marketing. Dennis had a new apple to talk about, and needed a partner in the venture. Many great companies came to mind, but when we shuffled through all of the prospects, I picked Stemilt. Yes, the same company that had been led by Tom Mathison. I suggested a meeting with West Mathison, who had just recently been named Tom's successor. West and Dennis hit it right off, and West grasped this new idea and wanted to pursue this venture. At the time of his passing, Tom was the largest investor in a new venture that will sell an apple under the trademark name of SweeTango.

Patience, persistence, and pushing through rejection finally paid off. Stemilt sells some of my cherries, as well as some of my apples packed through Douglas Fruit. We are now business partners.

Tom Mathison was not just a survivor, but the ultimate survivor. Blazing a trail for many of us, he has shown many growers how patience and persistence can prevail.

Kent Waliser
General Manager
Sagemoor

Tom, no one has taught me more than you. We have built so many things together over the years. I can still remember them all.

I started with you when the Hill plant was the only plant, and we would tear down the cherry line to seg apples and pears. Yes, I do remember wooden boxes. I remember the day I smashed my hand in the box maker and you had to drive me to town. It was a stupid way to get a week off in the middle of cherries. I spent many days rebuilding all those damn cherry bin trailers each spring. I was sure glad when you decided to sell them all.

When you appointed me to run the packing line on the Hill, I felt so honored that you had the confidence and trust in me to do the job.

When we moved to Olds Station and started to build the packing and shipping areas, this was a new challenge for me. We presized at Skookum for a year before we built a room and installed our own presizer. In the following years, we continued to build more cold rooms as we needed them.

I will never forget the time we were walking through the construction site at Olds when we were building rooms 10 to 17. Ron Cameron had put on the plans that no nail guns were to be used on his jobs. As we were walking, he saw a guy using a nail gun and he turned about three shades of red. He said, "look at this," and proceeded to kick a 4 x 8 sheet of MDO plywood off the wall, proving that the nails weren't hitting anywhere. After that, no more nail guns were used.

We had the opportunity to buy Columbia Street, Miller, and Chelan. This gave Stemilt the packing and cold storage we needed. It was fun and lot of hard work at the same time. There was a lot of clean up involved to make these old plants run efficiently.

Being out of town so much while building the Pasco facility was a challenge I had not encountered before. I drove home at night and was back in Pasco at 7 the next morning.

Tom, we had so many trips together. One in particular that I recall was the time we were driving up Blewett Pass in the winter. A car pulled right in front of you and we ended up doing two 360's! Fortunately, we missed the car. Neither of us ever talked about it. We just drove on.

I remember going fishing in Alaska with you, and other plant managers and owners. It helped to build good relationships that have been assets to me over the years.

The trips to Europe were very interesting, and we met a lot of good people and saw some innovative equipment. There was that time you sent me to Holland for seven days to look at fruit as it arrived, but the ship was five days late, so we had to stay several extra days. It was then that I learned to drive in Europe—another educational experience.

I learned from you very early on that it is your name on the box and what is inside the box should represent that. I went on a trip with several people from the Apple Commission, opening boxes to look at fruit from all over the country. Each time we would open a Stemilt box, I took great pride in knowing it would be right because of the pride you had instilled in us as a group.

You have helped me through good times and bad. I have always respected your judgment and you always treated me with respect. Thank you for all of the things you have done for me and my family.

Steve Shiflett
Friend, Grower, & Retired Stemilt Employee
Stemilt Growers, Inc.

I had the privilege of working with and knowing Tom for 45 years.

I was a young architect and civil engineering graduate from Washington State University. After graduation, my wife and I moved to southern California for a job opportunity. We moved back to the Northwest two years later for a job in Yakima with a firm designing and supervising construction projects in the fruit industry. Two years later, in 1962, we decided to gamble and open our own architectural/engineering professional office.

My previous jobs had brought me to Wenatchee to supervise construction jobs, and that's where I met Gale Richardson. After I had been in my own business for one year, Gale recommended me to Tom. Thanks, Gale–however, did you have to tell him I was starving and would work cheap?

Tommy and I had a lot in common. I was 31, he was 36. Money was tight for both of us, but we were honest and willing to work hard. Our first meeting, he invited me to come up to have lunch with him on Stemilt Hill at his mother's house. When I drove in, he told me that they had lost most of their cherry crop the night before. He wanted me to help him design 2 CA rooms. I was so nervous—how could he discuss building immediately after the cherry loss? He told me he had to diversify.

That was the beginning of our business relationship. When TK built the cherry packing room at Stemilt Hill, money was so tight that, to save on cost, I designed a canopy in front with a beam that had to be shored up in the middle with a column to hold the roof up during heavy snow load. When G.G. Richardson's crew was erecting the canopy, it fell down, and G.G. fired most of his crew. They had to get a new beam for the canopy.

There are so many stories I could tell. One that West, Tom's grandson, remembers is one I've conveniently forgotten. He says during one of my friendly disagreements with Tom, I threw the plans on the floor and left. Now, really, would an easy-going, congenial guy like me do that? West refers to me as the Professor. He must have had some pretty hard-nosed professors.

Tom and I didn't always agree on what course to take. When he bought six acres at Olds Station and wanted me to do a master plan, I told him he didn't have enough property. A couple of days later, I sent him a rough sketch of the master plan that added 10 more acres. Of course, you all know what acreage Stemilt sits on today.

When I did a study for Tom on whether he should presize or not, I told him he didn't have enough fruit to justify a presizer. He was upset with me and told me that he would get enough fruit—and he did.

Even after I retired, Tom was always available to see me anytime I called. If he was too busy to meet, he'd say, "Come on and take a ride with me." We'd look at fruit, deliver checks, talk about the industry, or just BS about our long business relationship and friendship. I will miss you, Tom. Tom and Lorraine will always have a special place in my heart.

Ron Cameron
Retired architect, engineer, and close friend

The first time I met Tom, I was on the sidewalk in front of the old church on Chelan Avenue. I had no idea who this ordinary-looking guy was. He just casually put his hand out and introduced himself, "Hi, I'm Tom Mathison." I had to go ask somebody who that was.

Tom didn't feel it was necessary to carry on about his accomplishments and he was right—those accomplishments spoke for themselves. He didn't look very special, but I soon learned that he was.

Tom and Lorraine joined this church in 1953. Tom was one of the partners who purchased the five-acre cherry orchard that was on this property, and then gave it to the church. That made it possible for us to build the current building which not only serves the church family, but the community as well.

One of my fondest memories of Tom involved golf. A few years ago, I commented to Tom that I wondered why he never invited me to play in the annual Stemilt golf tournament at the Highlander. I was just pulling his leg. Two months later, he informed me that I was in the next tournament! A few weeks after that, he told me I would be playing with him, Bob, and Hans. All of a sudden, a nonplayer is out there playing with the three kings! How nerve-wracking! The end of the story is I had a great time.

Tom had a great amount of grace. I never saw him under pressure. My perception is he was a humble, but powerful man. I never heard him bragging about his accomplishments, beyond something like, "We had a pretty good year."

Pastor Paul Pankey
First Presbyterian Church

When I first met Tom, I was in high school and came to Stemilt Hill to work on the cherry line during the summer. I remember each morning as he made his rounds through the shed, how everyone would be intimidated when he walked in. Nobody would talk or even look up from their jobs.

For years, I was of the same mind every time he came into the warehouse—that was, until I got to know him. I learned that this man, who seemed so cranky, was really a kind, caring, and very work-driven person. He had so many ideas constantly running through his mind that he didn't have time for a lot of chit-chat. But he did really care for his employees deeply. As time went on and I got to know him better, it was clearly evident that Tom thought his employees and growers were the best and Stemilt was growing to be the best because of them.

In an industry mainly driven by men, Tom always had faith in me and pushed me to climb the ladder in the company. If it wasn't for him, I wouldn't be where I am today. He encouraged me to enter Sales because he "just knew I could do it!" That was the best gift he ever gave to me—his encouragement and support through all these years. He would pass through the office, give me a hug, ask about Meijer (my account), and then tell me I was doing a good job. It still means so much to me.

Tom was also so supportive of me when I adopted my two girls from China. He always asked for updates as I was doing all the mounds of paperwork. I remember when I got off the Wenatchee plane with daughter Ali, Tom was there with others from Stemilt to welcome us home, and he was one of the first to hold her. He took photos and framed them, giving them to me as a gift for her homecoming.

Even with all of the big stuff he worried about at work, he always took time to ask about the kids and bring me box tops that Lorraine had saved for the school fundraisers.

I will always admire, respect, and miss him dearly. He was a great friend.

Wendy Everhart
Domestic Sales Manager
Stemilt Growers, Inc.

When I think of Tom, it is with much admiration. He was wise beyond his time. He never forgot things and could recall things from 70 years ago like it was yesterday.

Having worked for him for years was a pleasure. He had faith in how we ran our departments and would let us do that on our own, though he always loved to be asked, "Tom, what would you do in that situation?"

There were some things we could always count on with Tom:

- If he was out of town traveling on business, he would be sure to call at 5:00 p.m. to make sure we were still all working.
- If he saw fruit on his trip that he didn't like, we had better have it corrected by the time he got back.
- He liked to drive fast! If you ever got to drive and he was the passenger, the last thing you wanted him to tell you was "get that bat off your shoulder and swing!"
- He loved to have "kitchen cabinet" or "fireside" chats where he would take a few of us out to dinner to discuss our Stemilt problems or opportunities, and solve them that night.
- If there was a bank deposit of over $1 million, he better be the one to take it in.
- If you planned a birthday party for him, you might as well go ahead and start it without him. He wasn't much into celebrating his own birthdays, but he loved to celebrate those for others.

Tom was a very generous man. I got to go on many trips with employees to Maui, which Tom paid for out of his own pocket. He would take us out to dinner and spare no expense. He just enjoyed the company and talked about those trips for years.

He loved to help people and did so whenever he could. He loaned me money once when we were buying a new home and the sale of our other house had fallen through. The money for the new home was dependent on that sale, but Tom said, "Don't worry—let me loan you the money and then when your other house sells, pay me back."

I will never forget the day when Tom came into my office, all excited, telling me he had made a big decision. He announced he was only going to work part-time from now on! I thought this was great, coming from a man who worked from 5:00 a.m. to midnight at times, especially during cherry season. He would now have time to golf and get some well-deserved rest. Wrong! It meant he was only working from 8:00 a.m. to 8:00 p.m.! The idea of "reducing" his hours that way was exciting to him.

Diane Parker
Executive Office Manager
Stemilt Growers, Inc.

My dad, by nature, was a forward-thinking person. The definition of a problem is a start to a solution. The rest is just plain hard work. He was so occupied by the exciting life of the here and now, sometimes he forgot to say thank you. He assumed everyone knew how grateful he was to the people who were the solution to the problems. He would want me to thank every person in our community for participating in an adventure together:

- To all the farmers, teachers, scientists, and builders—thank you.
- To all the family members and neighbors—thank you.
- To all the orchard managers, and members of boards, committees, fact-finding tours, and marketing tours—thank you.
- To all of the people who visited Tom during his illness and sent prayers, and to his caregivers—thank you.
- To the doctors and all of the church family who gave us comfort—thank you.

Tom believed in God and he felt God believed in him. Only through God's grace did he have the instincts, perseverance, intelligence, and patience that his life adventure required of him.

Lavonne Mathison van Someren Gréve
Tom's daughter

I had the privilege of spending more than 20 years with Tom on a daily basis, and developing a friendship that touched my soul and will last the rest of my life.

I am, by training, a tax lawyer. Tom, extremely proud of his service to this country in the war, would say to me, "Peter, this is the greatest country on the face of the earth, and whatever we pay in taxes is worth it. We receive so much here that we could never pay enough!"

At the same time, he would ask me to make his payment as small as possible. However, he was grateful for everything he received.

Tom wanted me to deliver a special message to his family. He would sit in my office and, in his very humble way, he would almost confess that he was so disappointed in himself for having let family members down on an individual basis and on specific terms. He would turn to me and ask, "How do I let them know how much I love them and how proud I am of them? I'm so sorry that I didn't express this more often."

I heard him say this more than 100 times. He would bare his soul and tell me things because he knew they stayed in that confidential relationship.

Tom was an optimist, a worker, a perpetual motion machine. He never met a day, a challenge, or an obstacle that he could not embrace because he knew he had his family to get him through it. He was humbled to be so blessed. He would tell you, "Thank you for everything and keep going." Most importantly, he would tell you to help each other.

Tom would look outside, even on the worst day, and say there is hope in the air and spring is on its way. He would tell me, "Every day after the 22nd of December, the days will get longer." He would say each day is a wonderful day.

Peter Spadoni
Attorney
Jeffers, Danielson, Sonn, & Aylward PS

I met Tom Mathison in 1984 when I moved from Oregon to manage North Central Washington's commercial banking division for Rainier Bank, now known as Key Bank. Tom had moved his accounts across the street to Sea First Bank about six months prior to my arrival after he had been declined a loan by Rainier to expand Stemilt's CA storage capacity.

I reviewed the closed file and felt it was a loan the bank should have made. I called Tom and asked if he would have lunch with me. He said he would be available for a breakfast meeting at Smitty's restaurant, but warned me that it was very improbable that he would be able to work with Rainier Bank. He said the guys in Seattle didn't like him.

At that meeting, I asked Tom what he would like Stemilt to look like in five years if money was available. He gave me his wish list and I wrote it on a napkin. I told him I would like a chance to come up with a structure that would help him achieve that aggressive plan by restructuring his loans.

At a later lunch meeting, I shared a plan that injected funds for expansion and working capital. He liked the looks of the plan, but was sure it was not worth pursuing due to Seattle's dislike for him. He told me not to pursue the project, but he would give me a chance to test the water by helping him finance Bob and Kyle who were in the process of dividing up the orchards and setting up separate operations.

A year later, Tom called and said he was pleased with the bank's financing for the partnerships and was willing to let me try to put together the program for Stemilt that we had discussed the previous year, but he still doubted I would be able to get it approved.

Upon getting the approvals, we began a professional, as well as a personal, friendship that included dinners and golf outings that continued after I left the bank in 1991.

One of the last golf trips we took was to Canada. My sons, Todd and Lance, joined Tom and me playing two courses a day for three days. In Kelowna, British Columbia, on the way back to the motel after playing Predator Ridge—our second course for the day—we passed a golf course we had not scheduled to play. One of the boys jokingly commented that we could get nine holes in before dark. I assumed Tom would be tired and played out, but he said, "Let's do it." After three long days of golfing and late dinners where we sorted out the gambling debts from the games, we ended the trip with another game in Oliver, British Columbia on the way home.

During one of my last visits with Tom a couple of weeks prior to his death, he thanked me again for believing in him and Stemilt when he really needed help. We ended our visit with prayer.

Mel Hanson
Former Manager
Key Bank

I think of my Grandfather's life and I am amazed at how much God is all around us.

Armed with a passion for quality, Tom stood up to all of the strong forces. He had a plan to improve things, even though his plan fell on deaf ears and people of weak vision. Nothing stopped him, though. He built a one-room packing shed with a cold room. He made transitions from forklift driver, supervisor, salesperson, bookkeeper, manager. He learned to teach, mentor, guide, and lead people.

Now, Stemilt is driven by teams of empowered people who solve problems just like the ones Tom faced in the early days.

Tom inspires greatness.

West Mathison
President
Stemilt Growers, Inc.